everyday**genius** INSTITUTE

Companion Guide.

Meet **Tim Gaiser,**
Master Sommelier

Think like a Genius Wine Master.

Master wine tasting using the simply genius strategies of a world-class sommelier.

Table of Contents.

Introduction:
Go from wine lover, to wine genius.

How would you like to be able to select wines with confidence?

Imagine opening a bottle of wine and being able to identify it's age, it's quality and where it came from. Imagine being able to smell and taste the nuances of the wine and evaluate the quality and complexity.

When you are out to dinner with friends, you look through the wine list and easily select a great wine for the occasion. Your friends at the table are impressed with your ability to taste and evaluate the wine. They admire how you are able to make the right selection of wine for the right experience and food.

When you follow the steps in this guide, you will find that you can think like a genius sommelier. Not only will you be able to think like one, but you will be able to see, smell and taste like one. And with a bit of practice, you'll amaze yourself with your ability to taste wines in a whole new way.

By the time you've watched the video and experimented with the process here, you'll be able to evaluate any wine and be able to choose the right wine, for the right food and the right mood.

It doesn't take 20 years to learn this skill when you find out what one of the world's best wine tasters does consciously and subconsciously every time he tastes wine. When you adopt this incredible wine tasting strategy, you'll find that you become a much better wine taster, much faster.

Recommendation: Watch the video first.

Discover the simply genius strategy of Tim Gaiser.

Tim Gaiser is a genius wine taster. He is one of fewer than 200 people in the world to pass the most elite sommelier wine exam and earn the title of Master Sommelier. He is the Wine Education Chair for the prestigious Court of Master Sommeliers and teaches wine tasting at the very highest levels.

When you watch Tim taste wine, you feel as if you are watching magic happen. He looks at the wine, takes a quick sniff, then a quick taste and then tells you all about the wine as if he were the wine maker himself. It all happens in just a few seconds. We wanted to know how he does it, so we got inside his mind and figured out just what he does every time he tastes a wine.

What we discovered is so simple that it's genius. Here we'll show you his tasting strategy and how you can put his strategy into practice for yourself. You'll be amazed at how easy it is to learn.

Experience wine in a whole new way.

When you become a better wine taster, a whole new world of wine opens up to you. By adopting Tim's strategy you will be able to:

o   Identify all of the aromas and flavors in a wine
o   Evaluate the age, quality and complexity of a wine
o   Easily select the right wine, for the right food and the right mood
o   Impress your friends with your ability to taste and select wines
o   Take your wine tasting to the next level and enjoy wine even more

Learn Tim's 3-step tasting process.

When Tim evaluates a wine, he does three things:

See   Smell   Taste

After you have watched the video and read this guide thoroughly, you will learn each step in Tim's tasting process and be able to taste like a pro.

Notice how the same wine tastes different every time.

Before we begin, it's important to realize you are tasting a snapshot in time. You'll want to consider the wine from within the context or the setting. The same wine may taste different on another day or in another setting.

As you taste wine, be sure and consider the three variables:

o   **Wine** - temperature of the wine, how long it's been open, etc.
o   **Taster** - time of day you are tasting, what you are eating, your own body chemistry, etc.
o   **Setting** - the location, time of day, people you are with, etc.

Wine   Taster   Setting

If any of these variables change, the taste of the wine will change too. As you taste wine, think about the context and the variables. What do you notice about the wine? What do you notice about yourself? And what do you notice about the setting? These are important things to consider in your evaluation of the wine.

In the next step you will learn how to uncover secrets of the wine, just by looking at it.

Step 1:
See the wine.

Take a good look.

Looking at a wine is like looking at your plate of dinner as the waiter sets it down in front of you in a restaurant. As you look at your meal, you start to get a sense of what it's going to taste like and how good it will be before you've even taken a bite.

Looking at a wine is the same thing. Your eyes will start to tell you about the wine before you've even taken a sip. As you look at the wine, you can start to notice the alcohol content, the age of the wine, the grape variety and even the storage conditions. When you look at a wine, you are looking for:

o   Viscosity (tears or legs)
o   Color
o   How the wine compares against a baseline of others in your experience

Goals for looking at the wine.

As you look at the wine, your objectives are to:

o   Build expectations about the wine based only on what it looks like
o   Identify the color and use that information to identify age & grape variety
o   Determine viscosity (alcohol content or the presence of residual sugar)
o   Determine if there are any flaws (e.g., Cloudy? Color too dark? Too light?)
o   Visually compare against your mental baseline to assess the wine and also build up your
     mental wine library

A few basics.

Before you get started, there are a few wine tasting basics you should know. Be sure and:

o   Use good glassware (see below)
o   Fill the glass only 1/3 but never more than 1/2 full, otherwise you spill the wine when you swirl
     and don't get a full bouquet
o   Hold the glass by the stem, not the bowl
o   Look at the wine against a white background if possible

Good Glassware
Holds 14 oz.
Has a Cut Rim
Is Clear Crystal

Too full.

Fill the glass no more than 1/2 full.

Look at the viscosity (tears or legs).

Viscosity will tell you how much alcohol and/or residual sugar are in the wine. The amount of alcohol and residual sugar you see will help you start to build a picture of what the wine will taste like.

o **Lighter viscosity** – faster, thinner legs - means the wine is from a cooler climate and has less alcohol (and no residual sugar)

o **Richer viscosity** - slower, thicker legs – means higher alcohol and the grapes are grown in a warmer climate (there may be some residual sugar)

Faster, thinner legs
= less alcohol

Slower, thicker legs
= more alcohol

Look at the color.

The color of the wine will tell you the age and possibly the grape variety.

Age changes the color of the same wine. White and blush (pink) wines get darker with age while red wines do the opposite and get lighter with age.

White wines darken with age.

Red wines lighten with age.

Different grape varieties have different colors. There are many different colors of wine. For example, Pinot Noirs are often red in color while Cabernets are often dark burgundy.

The following picture shows the different colors you may find in the different types of wine.

The different colors of wine.

White	Rosé	Red
Straw	Pink	Brown
Yellow	Salmon	Garnet
Gold		Ruby Red
Brown	Brown	Purple

Compare the wine against a baseline.

As you look at the wine, notice how it compares against a visual baseline of similar wines in your experience. Notice what is the same or different in the wine you are looking at compared to a 'good' example of a wine of the same variety.

To compare a wine against your mental baseline, you must establish a baseline. In order to build a baseline, start by looking at 3 wines of the same variety. Look at the color and viscosity of those wines. Lock in the memory of the color and viscosity for that varietal.

To help you lock in your memory, look at the wines and give the color a name and say it out loud. For example, you could say "Pinot Noir, light red." And then do the same for the viscosity. For example, you might say, "Pinot Noir, medium-thick tears." Saying the words out loud and giving them a label will help you to remember the visual attributes of that grape varietal.

Build a baseline by comparing:

3 Chardonnays
3 Pinot Noirs

Genius Tip: Evaluate against baseline images.

Tim Gaiser is quickly able to gather a lot of information about the wine just by looking at it. When we modeled him, we discovered that he keeps baseline images in his mind and then compares the current wine he is tasting against a related baseline image.

Tim has coded into his memory a picture of what a great wine of a specific variety looks like. For example, he has a picture in his mind's eye of what a really great Pinot Noir looks like. In the mental image he has locked in the color, the viscosity and the clarity. He knows the region the wine came from and how it was stored. When he looks at a new wine, he compares what he sees to the mental image in his mind of that great baseline wine. This process allows him to notice what is the same or different. For example, if the current wine is a lighter color than the baseline image, he can often determine that the wine is older. Or if the tears are thicker than the baseline image, he can determine that the wine has more alcohol and is grown in a warmer climate than his baseline wine.

This is a very streamlined way to gather information about the wine. By holding these baseline images in his mind, he can scan his mental library quickly and then just notice things that are different from the baseline. By having a great wine to reference against, he can put the wine he is looking at into a category that he already understands. From there he can just notice what is unique about the current wine within that category.

Try this quick excercise: Take a moment and think about sitting inside of an expensive car such as a new Mercedes, Lexus or BMW. Notice the material on the seats, the features on the dashboard and the type of flooring. Now take a moment and think about sitting inside a cheap car. Notice the material on the seats, the features on the dashboard and the type of flooring. With these two images in your mind, notice what is different between the two. How do you evaluate the two cars in terms of quality? What are you paying attention to? Is it easy for you to recall images of these cars?

The same visual strategy can be used to compare wines. When you think about the components of wine, it helps to have a baseline of a quality wine against which to compare other wines. As you taste more wines, you can continue to adjust your own mental baseline and have more examples you can draw from. Like cars, each wine falls into a category. Within that category there are attributes that are similar (e.g., sedans, SUVs, sports cars) and things that are unique to each item in that category (e.g., seat material, dashboard features, electronics, flooring, etc.). Wine is the same way! Pinot Noirs fall into a category of wine. By noticing things like color, viscosity and clarity, you can start to notice the unique elements of each wine you taste in that category.

As humans we access visual memories by looking up and to the left. This is the location in the brain where remembered images are stored. You can use your eyes to both lock in and access baseline images for wine. Test it out. Think of the color of the last wine you tasted. Look up and to the left to recall the mental image in your mind. You will find that you can recall the image more easily when you look in this location. You can contrast this by trying to remember the color of the last wine you tasted by looking down and to your right. Can you recall the color when you look there? Chances are you won't be able to.

Step 1: See the wine.

Step 2:
Smell the wine.

Take a good sniff.

You've discovered some things about the wine by looking at it. Now it's time to smell it. Many wine experts believe that smelling the wine is the most important part of the entire tasting process. This is Tim's favorite part.

As a culture we don't generally place a high value on developing our sense of smell. However, you might be surprised to discover that you can learn to improve your sense of smell quite easily. In this step, we'll show you how to smell the wine. We'll also show you a method to improve your ability to smell and detect the different aromas in wine.

Goals for smelling the wine.

As you smell the wine, your objectives are to:

o   Determine the components in the wine: fruit, non-fruit, mineral/earth, oak
o   Determine if there any flaws. Is the wine corked? Oxidized?
o   Enjoy the smell of the wine and the sense of discovery

Smelling basics.

There's no consensus about the proper smelling technique. Some experts advocate two or three quick sniffs while others prefer one deep, sharp inhalation. Some tasters close one nostril, sniff, then close the other and sniff again. Play with it to see how you can get the most smell from the wine.

Before you smell, be sure and swirl the wine first. Swirling opens up the wine and intensifies the aromas.

When you smell the wine, hold the glass at a 30 - 45 degree angle to your face. Put your nose right in or near the glass. Some people find they can smell better by opening their mouth a little bit and breathing in and out gently using both nose and mouth.

Try smelling in different ways and notice what works best for you.

Glassware stance.
Hold the glass at a 30 - 45 degree angle to your face.

Look for these four things when you smell the wine.

When you smell the wine, there are 4 things to smell for:

o   Fruits
o   Non-fruits (such as floral qualities, herbs or spices)
o   Mineral/Earth (such as earth/dirt, rocks or leaves)
o   Oak

Better wines are more complex and have more components. Use this wine component grid to remind you of the four components to look for in the wine.

Fruits

Non-Fruits

Earth/Mineral

Oak

How to smell the wine, step-by-step.

Tim smells wine by linking up his nose with his eyes. He literally makes a mental picture of each component in the wine he smells. He places all of these pictures into a visual collage. As you smell the wine, build your own visual collage of what you notice in the wine. Here is his step-by-step smelling procedure:

1. Get really present to the wine and focus.
2. Smell the wine. Get curious and ask yourself 'What's there?'
3. Smell first for fruits. They are often the most dominant smell.
4. As you smell, make a mental picture of first thing you notice (such as apple). put that image in your visual collage, hold it and then go back to the wine.
5. Ask yourself again, 'What else is there?' and notice something else in the wine. Smell BEYOND the apple and notice what else is there. Once you identify something else (such as lemon), put that image on your visual collage and hold it there. Go back to the wine again. You now want to smell beyond the apple and lemon and notice what else is in the wine.
6. Repeat this process until you have smelled for fruits, non-fruits, earth/mineral and oak and have created a full collage of all of the elements in that wine.

Build a visual collage of things you smell in the wine.

Hold smell #1.   Ask'What's there?'   Ask'What's there?'   Ask'What else?'
                  Hold smell #2.   Hold smell #3.

Smell beyond each element and see what else is there.

When you make a picture of something you smell and hold that picture in your mind's eye, you can smell beyond that initial element. With these pictures clear in your mind, you will remember what you've already smelled and you can go back to the wine to notice even more. Great wines have many subtle aromas. This procedure allows you to keep noticing more and more subtle parts of the wine. Also, some wines may have a very overpowering aroma. By attending to the powerful aroma and holding the image, you can smell beyond it and find out what else is in the wine. As you first learn this process, you may find you need to smell the wine a number of times to notice everything that is in the wine. As you get more practice, you will get faster.

Notice how you organize items in your visual collage.

Tim creates his visual collage by placing items from left to right, like this:

Fruits   Non-Fruits   Earth/Mineral   Oak

Try his way of organizing, but change it around if you find another way that is easier for you.

Note any problems.

Corked: Sometimes wines have bad corks, which contaminate the wine. Corked wine has an odor resembling a moldy newspaper, damp cloth, or damp basement.

Oxidized: Sometimes a wine has been significantly exposed to air (oxygen), thereby changing its aroma and flavor. Fully oxidized wines have a tired, spoiled flavor. An oxidized white wine usually has begun to turn brown.

A proven method to improve your smelling ability.

The fastest way to get better at wine tasting is to train your nose. The way to train your nose is to smell different fresh fruits, dried fruits, vegetables, spices, earth components and oak. As you smell something, immediately make a mental picture of what you are smelling and say the name of it out loud. The goal here is to link a smell with a mental image and a name of that item.

Go to your refrigerator, spice rack, garden or grocery store to practice. Train your nose until you can easily make a mental picture of the item you smell. Some people find it helpful to close their eyes so they can more fully focus on the smell and the single picture. Take one fruit and smell it 20 times using this process. You'll be able to lock it into memory in about 5 minutes.

To remember what things smell like:

To remember what things smell like, you must make it important and practice linking smells with mental pictures.

Smell an item.

Make a mental picture of what you are smelling.

Say the name of it out loud.

Apple

Train your nose to recognize these common wine smells:

Wine Component	Common White Wine Smells	Common Red Wine Smells
Fruit	• Apples • Pears • Lemon • Lime • Grapefruit • Peach • Pineapple Note: Smell both fresh and dried fruits!	• Blackberries • Black cherry • Red cherry • Cranberry • Black currant • Plums • Red Raspberry • Banana • Jam • Dried Prune • Dried Fig • Raisins Note: Smell both fresh and dried fruits!
Non-Fruit	• Butter • Rose • White flowers • Honey • Toast • Almond • Orange blossoms	• Violets • Black & White Pepper • Green Bell Pepper • Lavender • Mint • Leather
Earth/Mineral	• Mineral • Chalk • Wet rocks	• Barnyard • Dirt/earth • Wet leaves • Mushroom • Must • Dust
Oak	• Smokey • Wood • Oak • Toast • Vanilla • Baking spices	• Smokey • Wood • Oak • Toast • Vanilla • Baking spices

Genius Tip: Notice how you code smells.

As human beings we filter our experiences through our five senses. We use our visual sense, auditory sense, kinesthetic sense, olfactory sense (sense of smell) and gustatory sense (sense of taste). These are the "modalities" of experience. We can make even finer distinctions in these five modalities. For example, in the visual modality we can make distinctions such as brightness, size, magnification, color or black and white, location, distance, contrast and much more. We call these finer distinctions "submodalities."

When Tim Gaiser smells wine, he is using the visual modality to recognize smells. He makes vivid mental pictures of the elements he smells. His brain links a smell with an image in his mind's eye. This image has submodality distinctions such as size, brightness, location, distance, movement, background, frames and more. In other words, when Tim slows down his smelling process, he notices that his mind makes mental pictures in a way that helps him to detect and remember the aromas in the wine.

Through years of research we have discovered that nearly everyone makes mental pictures when they smell something. Often our minds create these pictures at lightning speed so we never really notice it. However, if you slow down your own thought process, you will begin to notice how your own mind codes smell. Understanding how your own brain codes smells - by noticing the submodalities of the mental pictures you create - will make a huge difference in your ability to detect and remember aromas.

Try this quick excercise: Imagine you have a lemon in your hand. Take an imaginary sniff of the lemon. As you do, notice what image your mind creates as you smell. You will need to slow down your thought process and really become aware of what your mind is doing to recognize the smell. As you do this, ask yourself these questions to determine the submodalities of your mental image:

-What image appears in your mind's eye as you think of smelling a lemon?
-Is the picture still or moving?
-Is is flat or three dimensional?
-Where is the image located? Near, far, to the right, to the left?
-Is it in color or black and white?
-Is it bright or dim?
-Is it sharp focus or fuzzy?
-Is there a border around the image or not?

Once you become aware of the images your mind creates when you smell something and notice the submodalities, you will be well along the path to becoming a better taster. You can consciously train your nose by smelling an item, noticing the details of the mental picture you create, and linking the name of the item to the picture. In this way you are using multiple sensory systems to recognize and recall smells.

Tim Gaiser suggests that beginners link a memory to a smell. For example, when smelling strawberries, linking that smell to a visual memory of strawberry shortcake your grandmother made one 4th of July can be a powerful way to code the smell in your mind.

Step 3:
Taste the wine.

Take a good sip.

You have seen and smelled the wine. Now it's time to taste it. Tasting the wine is often the part that people like best. The tasting process is a confirmation of what you've noticed on the nose, plus an analysis of a few additional structural elements.

Goals for tasting the wine.

As you taste the wine, your objectives are to:

o   Confirm each of the elements you smelled
o   Assess the wine's structure by evaluating: acid, alcohol, tannin and finish
o   Check for balance (how the components interact and change in your mouth) and harmony
         (how all of the components work together)
o   Assess the complexity and quality

What are the structural elements in wine?

In the tasting process you are evaluating 4 additional structural elements. They are:

Acid: The agreeable tart or sour taste caused by natural fruit acids. In moderate amounts acidity balances any wine and is a favorable characteristic.

Alcohol: The result of fermentation of sugars by yeast. In the wine industry, alcohol specifically refers to ethyl alcohol that you can sense as heat in the bridge of your nose, throat or chest cavity.

Tannin or Tannic Acid: Tannin is a natural component found in the skins, seeds and stems of grapes. It is most prominent in red wines, especially young reds, where it creates a dry, puckering sensation in the mouth. Tannin in wine mellows with age and eventually drops out of the wine to form sediment. Tannin is also a natural preservative and a necessary component for any red wine to age.

Finish: The finish is simply the after taste of a wine or the impression left in the mouth after you have swallowed the wine. To be good, it should be distinctive and memorable rather than watery, short (the flavor isn't sustained), or bitter and astringent. Tim thinks of the finish in terms of length along a line with a vanishing point.

Structural elements.

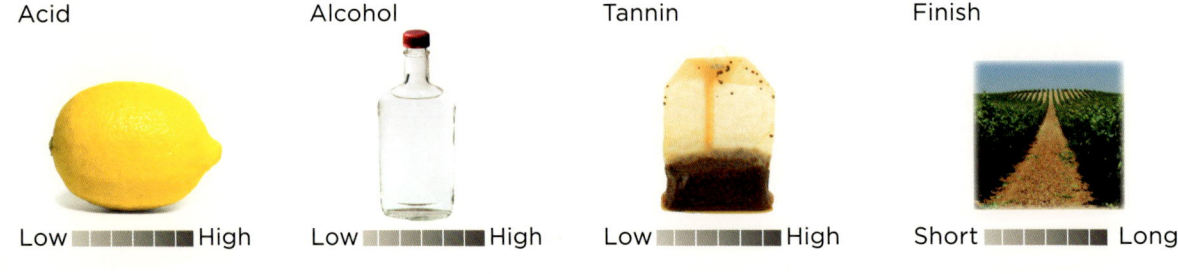

Acid
Low ▨▨▨▨▨ High

Alcohol
Low ▨▨▨▨▨ High

Tannin
Low ▨▨▨▨▨ High

Finish
Short ▨▨▨▨▨ Long

Tasting basics.

Getting the most taste out of the wine requires you to really swish the wine around inside of your mouth. When you taste the wine:

o   Swirl the wine in the glass to open up the bouquet
o   Take a sip of the wine – not too much!
o   Coat the inside of your mouth with the wine as completely as you can
o   After you swallow (or spit), suck in a bit of air to get a last impression of the wine

How to taste the wine, step-by-step.

The tasting procedure is similar to the smelling procedure. You want to notice what's in the wine and add that element to your visual collage. To taste the wine:

1.   Swirl, sip, coat your mouth, suck in a bit of air and ask "What's there?"

2.   Compare what you taste to what you already smelled and placed in your visual collage (fruits, non-fruits, earth/mineral and oak). Notice the taste of each component you smelled. Make any necessary adjustments to your visual collage (you may need to add or remove items).

3.   Re-taste the wine again and notice the structural elements: acid, alcohol, tannin and finish. Notice these elements one by one. Add the elements you notice in the wine to your visual collage.

4.   Re-taste again and look for balance and harmony. Is anything too strong or delicate? Are all of the elements working together?

5.   Use all of the information you see, smell and taste and use that to assess the quality and complexity of the wine.

6.   Complete your visual collage.

TIP: Some people like to add a visual of the wine label to their collage. Try it!

TIP: If you take your visual collage and 'move it up' in your field of vision so that you are looking UP at it, that will help lock in the memory of the wine. Most people access visual memories by looking up and to their left, so that's a good place to move your mental picture so it's locked into your memory.

Taste the wine at least 3 times.

Taste to confirm smells.

When you taste, the first thing to do is compare what you taste to what you already smelled. Notice the fruits, non-fruits, earth/mineral and oak. Take each item in your visual collage and notice that element in the taste.

Fruits

Non-Fruits

Earth/Mineral

Oak

Retaste to evaluate structure.

Retaste the wine and notice the acid, alcohol and tannins (if any) in the wine. Notice the length of the finish. Add each item you notice to your visual collage.

Acid

Low ▨▨▨▨▨▨ High

Alcohol

Low ▨▨▨▨▨▨ High

Tannin

Low ▨▨▨▨▨▨ High

Finish

Short ▨▨▨▨▨▨ Long

Retaste to assess balance & harmony.

Retaste the wine and look for balance (how the components interact and change in your mouth) and harmony (how all of the components work together). Adjust your visual collage to reflect how you would represent the blanace and harmony of the elements in the wine.

Balance   Harmony

Complete your visual collage.

When you have finished seeing, smelling and tasting the wine, you will have a full mental collage of that wine. Each person's collage will look a little different.

Here is an example of Tim's wine collage from the video. He places the structural elements below the main wine components. Your collage may be organized differently!

A proven method to improve your tasting ability.

You can improve your tasting ability in the same way you can improve your smelling ability. Taste different components (fruits, non-fruits, earth/mineral and oak) and different structural elements (acid, alcohol, tannin and finish) and make pictures of what you taste. You want to make a link between what you taste and a picture of that element and the name. Practice on anything you taste, including any foods or liquids. Look at the Common Wine Smells chart in this guide for a list of things to taste. For the Structural Elements, the best practice is to taste wine!

Taste an item.

Make a mental picture of what you are tasting.

Say the name of it out loud.

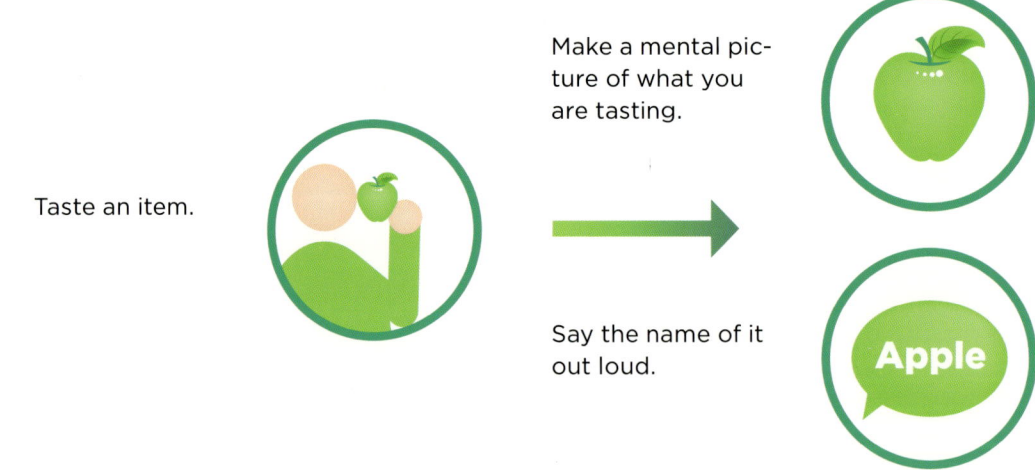

Genius Tip: Use mental templates.

We've discovered that Geniuses have highly streamlined processes and operate from a finite set of things that work for them every time. When Tim tastes wine, he pulls from a set of templates that he keeps in his mind. He keeps several lists in his head and pulls from the lists quickly and easily as he goes through each part of the tasting process. Tim uses mental templates for seeing, smelling and tasting.

Tim has a list of things he is looking for in the wine. He runs through his mental list and checks for:
  -Color
  -Viscosity
  -Clarity

As he smells the wine, he runs through his mental list and checks for:
  -Fruits
  -Non-Fruits
  -Earth/Mineral
  -Oak
  -Flaws

And finally, as he tastes the wine, he runs through his mental list and evaluates the wine for:
  -Acid
  -Alcohol
  -Tannin
  -Finish
  -Balance & Harmony

As Tim tastes wine, he quickly runs through his mental checklists and evaluates the wine for each component on the list. He then fills in a visual template in his mind's eye of each element he discovers in the wine. His visual template is highly organized and he has a placeholder for each mental picture he creates. Tim organizes his visual collage from left to right, then front to back. For example, when he smells the wine, he places fruits on the left, then stacks in different fruits he smells from front to back.

Create your own mental templates and organize your visual collage in a way that works best for you. Take the time to lock in the mental checklists and create placeholders in your mind's eye for each element you discover. Once you become aware of how you generate mental pictures, you'll be amazed at how well this process works and how fun and easy it is to taste wine in this way.

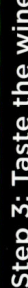

Food and Wine Pairing
Strategies to make everything taste better.

It's easier than you think!

Now that you know how to taste wine, the next step is to learn strategies that will help you pair wine and food together. By following a few key principles, you will be able to make the right selection of wine for the right food and the right mood.

When it comes to food and wine pairing, Tim Gaiser says there are four main combinations and three special cases to remember. Once you commit these combinations to memory you will have the information you need to select wines with confidence.

These are guidelines! Experiment with your own taste and remember that personal preference is more important than any pairing 'rule.'

Four main combinations.

When it comes to pairing wine with food, there are four main combinations.

Heat needs sweet.

Spicy food like Mexican, Middle Eastern, Thai.

Off-dry Riesling
Chenin Blanc
White Zinfandel

Acid needs acid.

Vinaigrettes or sauces with fresh citrus juices.

Sauvignon Blanc
Dry Riesling
Albariño or Pinot Grigio

Fats and proteins need tannin.

Red meat such as beef or lamb.

Cabernet & Cabernet Blends
Shiraz
Zinfandel

Sweet needs sweet.

Dishes with sweet sauces or fruit elements.

Slightly-to-medium sweet Riesling
Chenin Blanc
Muscat

Food and wine pairing.

Three special cases.

People often wonder what to pair with chicken, fish, cheese and dessert. These guidelines will help.

Chicken and fish.

Pair the wine based on the intensity of the preparation or sauce. Delicate preparations such as poaching or baking need a less intense wine. More intense preparations such grilling need a more intense wine. The richness or intensity of the sauce may also dictate the choice of wine.

Pair high acid whites (Sauvignon Blanc, Dry Riesling) with more delicate preparations such as poaching, baking or sautéing.

With more intense preparations such as grilling try richer whites with oak such as Chardonnay or medium-bodied reds such as Pinot or Merlot.

Cheese.

The butterfat and low acid in most cheeses require a high acid white with a touch of residual sweetness. Goat cheeses are the exception.

Slightly sweet Riesling such as German Spätlese. Try a crisp Sauvignon Blanc with goat cheese.

Desserts.

Be sure the dessert wine is always sweeter than the dessert.

Dessert-styled Riesling, Sauvignon Blanc, Sémillon, Muscat or sweet fortified wines such as Port, Sherry and Madeira.

Conclusion:
Now go pour yourself a glass of wine.

You are on the path to wine genius.

Congratulations! You now know how to taste wine like a pro. Once you've used this method and experienced for yourself how easy it is, you will find you are able to enjoy and evaluate wines in a whole new way.

Start training your nose and your palate! You will be amazed at how quickly you improve when you practice smelling and tasting.

Now go get a bottle of wine. Open it up. Pour yourself a glass and evaluate the wine using each step in this process. You will be surprised at what you discover.

Cheers!

The Core Strategies of Genius:
How to become a better wine taster using 7 proven techniques.

Unlock your inner genius.

Our Core Strategies of Genius product includes seven proven techniques that will help you to truly learn this wine tasting strategy. On the next two pages we provide a brief overview of each technique and share ideas on how you can apply these processes to significantly improve your own tasting ability. As you thoroughly read through how each of these strategies can help you, you will discover how easy it is to install this wine tasting strategy for yourself.

Core Strategies of Genius Technique	How you can use this technique to become a better wine taster.

WELL FORMED GOALS:
Achieve more in less time

Tim Gaiser is a great wine taster because he has clear goals he operates from when he tastes wine. You will naturally become a better taster by getting clear on your own goals.

The Well Formed Goal process will help you effectively set goals so that your conscious and subconscious behaviors automatically support your efforts. This is a goal setting strategy modeled from people who are highly effective at setting and achieving goals. It's unlike any goal setting process you've ever seen. Using this process will get you powerful results that may even surprise you.

NEW BEHAVIOR GENERATOR:
Install a new habit easily

Learning a genius process, like wine tasting, often requires remembering to do new things. The New Behavior Generator is a way to program yourself now to remember later. You can use this technique to make each part of the wine tasting strategy your own. Use this process to instantly lock in and remember the steps of the strategy. Use it to automatically remember what to see, smell and taste in the wine. You will be amazed at how quickly you improve when you use this technique.

PIECE OF CAKE:
Make it easy to learn

Because we don't realize how simple it can be to learn something new, we often give up before we master it. Using the Piece of Cake process will make your journey to become a better wine taster much more fun and easy. Use this technique to make training your nose and palette a piece of cake. Use it to make remembering wines easy.

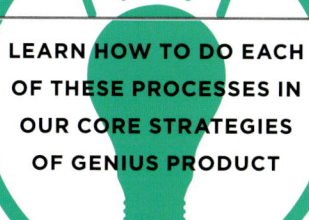

LEARN HOW TO DO EACH OF THESE PROCESSES IN OUR CORE STRATEGIES OF GENIUS PRODUCT

Core Strategies of Genius Technique	How you can use this technique to become a better wine taster.
 **EYE MOVEMENT INTEGRATION:** Eliminate feelings of anxiety, frustration or fear	Although it may seem a little strange, this process will help you eliminate any feelings of frustration, fear, self doubt or lack of confidence as you learn to taste wine. It's quick and easy to do and uses your own neurology so that you can use more of your brain power to break through any limitations to your own success. You can also use this technique to help you access your best mental state so you can be an even better wine taster.
 **MENTAL MENTORS:** Receive helpful advice from people you respect	Most of us have had people in our lives who have believed in us. They offer us useful advice, a new perspective or get us to consider something we hadn't thought of. The Mental Mentor process will give you a way to get insights that may not have occurred to you on your own. Take advantage of expert knowledge that is a part of your own mental processing and improve your tasting ability.
 **CIRCLE OF EXCELLENCE:** Step into powerful emotional states on demand	Circle of Excellence is a way to quickly and easily step into your most powerful mental state. This process will teach you how to do that on demand. You can build a Circle of Excellence to be at your best, most curious and present state when tasting wine. You can also use this process to create a powerful learning state as you train your eyes, nose and palate.
 **MOTIVATION STRATEGY:** Feel highly motivated to accomplish a task	This process will teach you how to easily motivate yourself to practice various aspects of wine tasting. It will allow you to make learning expert wine tasting a fun and enjoyable experience.

About Tim Hallbom, our genius modeler.

Tim Hallbom is a world-renowned behavioral scientist. He has mastered the process of deconstructing how geniuses are thinking.

Tim is able to get inside the minds of genius by asking a series of unique questions that bring out conscious and subconscious behaviors, patterns and actions. He observes eye movements, body language, speech patterns and voice tonality. He gets geniuses to slow down their thought processes so that he can understand their strategy, step-by-step. He then puts their process into a simple methodology that you can apply in your own life to get the same results.

Tim Hallbom worked with Tim Gaiser to uncover his wine tasting strategy. By using his proven modeling process he was able to help Tim Gaiser really figure out what he was doing inside his mind every time he tasted a wine. The video and companion guide here feature Tim Gaiser's process.

About us.

At the Everyday Genius Institute, we take people who are exceptional at what they do, deconstruct their process and then teach you exactly how you can get the same results.

In our Think Like a Genius series, we reveal for the first time exactly how geniuses are thinking and then teach you how to do the same. By modeling the strategies of the best in the world, you will unlock your inner genius, cut years off your learning curve and achieve mastery easier than you ever imagined.

To learn more about us and the strategies of genius we've deconstructed on topics ranging from wine tasting to sales, go online and visit us at **www.everydaygeniusinstitute.com**

v 2.0

Notes:

Notes: